Mindful Meditation for Depression: Cultivating Inner Peace and Healing

THOMAS M RODRIGUEZ III

Other books by Thomas

Available on Amazon

Leave a 1-Click Review!

I would be incredibly thankful if you could take just 60 seconds to write a brief review on Amazon, even if it's just a few sentences!

>> Click here to leave a quick review

DEDICATION

I am dedicating this book to everyone suffering from depression. I truly hope that if they don't come across this book that they somehow learn the tools to overcome their depression. I know the struggle all too well. I also ask if you know someone else caught in the web of depression that you pass this on to them or even better teach them what you learn in this book.

CONTENTS

ACKNOWLEDGMENTS

Anyone can greatly benefit from the help of others at times and in this fact I am no different. Having stated this I must acknowledge this book couldn't have been written without people such as Thich Naht Hanh, Lama Yeshe and the venerable Robina Cortin. It is through their knowledge and wisdom, as well as others that I gained my own.

INTRODUCTION

Depression has become a prevalent and pressing concern in our modern world, affecting millions of individuals across diverse backgrounds. It casts a shadow on our lives, draining our energy, distorting our thoughts, and dampening our spirits. While conventional treatments such as therapy and medication play vital roles in managing depression, there is a growing recognition of the transformative power of mindfulness-based practices, particularly mindful meditation, in alleviating its grip.

In this book, "Mindful Meditation for Depression: Cultivating Inner Peace and Healing," we embark on a journey of self-discovery, resilience, and healing. Here, we explore the profound practice of mindful meditation, specifically tailored to address the challenges and complexities of depression. Drawing from ancient wisdom and contemporary scientific research, we will uncover the tools and insights needed to cultivate inner peace, foster self-compassion, and navigate through the darkness of depression toward the light of well-being.

Throughout these pages, we will delve into the foundations of mindful meditation, understanding its principles and the scientific evidence supporting its efficacy in managing depression. We will learn how to establish a meditation practice, create a harmonious environment, and overcome common obstacles that may arise along the way. Guided by experienced practitioners and researchers in the field, we will explore various meditation techniques, such as breath awareness, body scan, and loving-kindness meditation, that have shown promising results in Reducing depressive symptoms.

But this book goes beyond the cushioned seat of meditation. It emphasizes the integration of mindfulness into our daily lives, infusing our routines, relationships, and self-care practices with a gentle, non-judgmental awareness. We will discover how mindful movement, such as yoga or walking meditation, can complement seated meditation and foster a deeper connection with our bodies. We will explore strategies to work with difficult emotions, resistance, and self-critical thoughts, transforming them into sources of compassion and growth.

It is crucial to acknowledge that mindful meditation is not a panacea or a quick fix for depression. It requires patience, commitment, and self-compassion. Yet, as we embark on this journey, we open the door to a profound transformation—a transformation that allows us to cultivate resilience, nurture well-being, and rediscover the inherent strength and wisdom within us.

As we embark on this exploration of mindful meditation for depression, let us remember that we are not alone on this path. By embracing the power of mindfulness and compassion, we tap into a collective wisdom that spans generations. Together, we will navigate the complexities of depression, one breath at a time, as we cultivate inner peace, healing, and a renewed zest for life.

May this book serve as a guiding light, illuminating the path toward a life of greater well-being and offering solace to those seeking relief from the shadows of depression.

CHAPTER 1: UNDERSTANDING DEPRESSION

Depression is much more than a simple bout of the blues. It is a pervasive and relentless sense of gloom that impacts your thoughts, feelings, and actions. It can make life seem laborious, draining the color and joy from your days. In this chapter, we delve into the depths of depression, exploring its various forms, common symptoms, causes, and the significant role of the mind-body connection in this disease.

Firstly, let's define depression. The American Psychiatric Association characterizes depression, or major depressive disorder, as a common and serious medical illness that negatively affects how you feel, the way you think, and how you act. It's not a sign of weakness or a negative personality. It is a significant public health issue that affects millions worldwide.

There are various forms of depression, each with its unique characteristics. Major Depressive Disorder (MDD), the most common form, is characterized by persistent feelings of sadness or lack of interest in outside stimuli. People with MDD may experience changes in appetite and weight, difficulties sleeping or sleeping too much, fatigue, loss of energy, feelings of worthlessness or excessive guilt, difficulty concentrating, and recurrent thoughts of death or suicide.

In addition to MDD, there are other forms of depression that deserve attention. Persistent Depressive Disorder (Dysthymia) is

characterized by a chronic depressed mood that lasts for at least two years. While the symptoms may be less severe than in MDD, they are long-lasting and can greatly impact daily functioning. Postpartum Depression is a severe form of depression that can affect new mothers following childbirth. It is often accompanied by feelings of sadness, anxiety, and exhaustion, making it challenging for mothers to care for themselves and their babies. Seasonal Affective Disorder (SAD) is another type of depression that usually occurs during the winter months when there is less natural sunlight. People with SAD experience symptoms such as low mood, loss of interest, increased sleep, and carbohydrate cravings.

Recognizing the common symptoms and signs of depression is the first step in seeking help. These signs include a consistent sad or anxious mood, feelings of worthlessness, decreased energy, difficulty concentrating, changes in sleep and appetite, and recurrent thoughts of death or suicide. It's important to remember that these symptoms can vary in intensity and frequency from person to person. No two experiences with depression are identical, which underscores the need for personalized care and treatment.

The causes and contributing factors of depression are complex and multifaceted, often encompassing a blend of genetic, biological, environmental, and psychological factors. Depression can run in families, suggesting a genetic link, but it often occurs in people with no family history of the illness. This indicates that genetic predisposition is not the sole determining factor. Life events such as trauma, loss of a loved one, a difficult relationship, early childhood trauma, or high stress can trigger episodes of depression. Additionally, certain medical conditions can risk depression, such

as vitamin D deficiency, thyroid problems, or chronic pain. It is important to approach depression holistically, considering all of these factors when seeking treatment and support.

Lastly, we'll highlight the mind-body connection in depression. Scientific research has revealed a strong link between the mind and body in depression. Depression has been linked to inflammation, changes in the body's stress response, and physiological changes in the brain. Furthermore, depression can lead to physical symptoms such as headaches, digestive disorders, and chronic pain. This mind-body connection is a crucial aspect of depression, reinforcing that it's not solely a mental or emotional condition but a systemic one that impacts your overall health.

Research has shown that depression can cause significant changes in the body's physiology. People with depression often have elevated levels of stress hormones such as cortisol, which can impact the immune system and increase inflammation in the body. Additionally, depression can lead to changes in the heart rate and blood pressure, disrupt sleep, and affect the
body's metabolic processes, which can contribute to weight gain or weight loss.

Moreover, the mind-body connection in depression is not just a one-way street. Just as the mind can impact the body, the body can also influence the mind. Physical illnesses or conditions, lack of exercise, poor diet, and sleep disturbances can all exacerbate symptoms of depression. Research has suggested that physical activity can help reduce symptoms of depression by boosting mood-enhancing chemicals in the brain like endorphins. Similarly, a balanced diet rich in fruits, vegetables, lean proteins, and whole grains can help maintain stable blood sugar levels, which can impact mood.

This mind-body connection underscores the importance of not just treating the mind in depression but also the body. This holistic approach can have a profound impact on the healing process, and it is the path we will be exploring throughout this book.

Understanding depression is the first step towards recovery. As we move forward in this book, we will explore how mindfulness meditation can be a powerful tool in managing depression, reducing its symptoms, and cultivating inner peace and healing. Mindfulness, as we will see, encompasses not just the mind but also the body, fostering a deeper sense of connection with ourselves and the world around us. This chapter lays the groundwork for this exploration, setting the stage for a comprehensive look at how the practice of mindfulness can be a beacon of hope in the darkness of depression.

Depression is a complex and often misunderstood illness, but it is also treatable. With a better understanding of the various forms of depression, the common symptoms, the myriad causes, and the significant mind-body connection, you are better equipped to embark on your journey towards healing. Hold onto this knowledge as we delve deeper into the world of mindfulness meditation and its potential for cultivating inner peace and healing from depression.

CHAPTER 2: THE FOUNDATION OF MINDFUL MEDITATION

In this chapter, we will delve into the foundations of mindful meditation, exploring its principles, origins, and the scientific evidence supporting its benefits for mental health, particularly in relation to depression. We will also discuss the importance of establishing intention and commitment to a meditation practice. By understanding these fundamental aspects, you will be equipped with the knowledge and motivation necessary to embark on your journey of cultivating inner peace and healing through mindful meditation.

Section 1: The Concept of Mindfulness and its Benefits for Mental Health

Defining Mindfulness:

Mindfulness can be described as the practice of intentionally paying attention to the present moment without judgment. It involves bringing a curious and non-reactive awareness to one's thoughts, emotions, bodily sensations, and the surrounding environment. Mindfulness invites us to observe our experiences without getting caught up in them or trying to change them.

Benefits of Mindfulness for Mental Health:

Research has shown that incorporating mindfulness into our lives can have a profound impact on our mental well-being. By developing a mindful approach, we can cultivate greater resilience, emotional regulation, and overall psychological well-being. Some of the specific benefits of mindfulness for mental health include:

- Reducing stress and anxiety: Mindfulness practices help to calm the nervous system and reduce the physiological and psychological effects of stress. By becoming more aware of our thoughts and reactions, we can respond to stressors with greater composure and clarity.

- Enhancing emotional regulation: Mindfulness allows us to observe our emotions without becoming overwhelmed by them. By developing a non-judgmental attitude towards our feelings, we can respond to them in more constructive and compassionate ways.

- Improving focus and attention: Mindfulness practices train our attention to stay focused on the present moment. This enhances our ability to concentrate, improves our productivity, and reduces mind-wandering and distractibility.

- Cultivating self-compassion and acceptance: Mindfulness us to approach ourselves and our experiences with kindness and acceptance. This fosters a sense of self-compassion and self-care, reducing self-criticism and promoting a more positive relationship with ourselves.

- Promoting resilience and coping skills: Mindfulness equips us with tools to navigate life's challenges with greater resilience. By cultivating present-moment awareness, we can respond to difficulties with clarity, adaptability, and a deeper understanding of ourselves.

Section 2: Origins and Principles of Mindful Meditation

Historical Roots:

Mindful meditation has its roots in ancient contemplative practices, particularly in Buddhist traditions such as Vipassana and Zen. These traditions emphasize the cultivation of mindfulness as a means to gain insight into the nature of reality and alleviate suffering. The teachings of mindfulness have been passed down through generations, and in recent decades, they have been adapted and integrated into secular contexts.

The Four Foundations of Mindfulness:

The teachings of mindful meditation often revolve around the Four Foundations of Mindfulness. These foundations provide a framework for developing mindfulness in various aspects of our experience. They are:

a) Mindfulness of the Body: This foundation involves bringing attention to bodily sensations, breath, and physical postures. By observing the body with non-judgmental awareness, we develop a deeper connection with our physical being and cultivate a sense of embodied presence.

b) Mindfulness of Feelings: In this foundation, we observe and recognize pleasant, unpleasant, and neutral feelings without

clinging to or aversion. We become aware of the changing nature of our feelings and develop a greater understanding of the transient and impermanent nature of our emotional experiences.

c) Mindfulness of the Mind: This foundation focuses on becoming aware of thoughts, emotions, and mental states as they arise and pass. We cultivate a non-reactive and non-identifying attitude towards our thoughts, allowing them to come and go without getting entangled in them. By observing the fluctuations of the mind, we develop a clearer understanding of our patterns of thinking and gain insight into the nature of our own consciousness.

d) Mindfulness of Phenomena: This foundation expands our awareness to external objects, such as sounds, sights, and experiences. We observe the world around us with a sense of curiosity and non-judgment, recognizing the interconnectedness of all phenomena. By developing a deep presence in our interactions with the world, we cultivate a sense of interconnectedness and interdependence.

Section 3: Scientific Evidence behind Mindfulness-based Approaches to Depression

Mindfulness-Based Cognitive Therapy (MBCT):

MBCT is an evidence-based approach that combines elements of cognitive therapy with mindfulness practices. It has been specifically designed to prevent relapse in individuals with recurrent depression. Research studies have demonstrated its

effectiveness in reducing depressive symptoms and enhancing overall well-being. MBCT helps us develop a new relationship with our thoughts and emotions, allowing us to respond to depressive patterns with greater awareness and self-compassion.

Neuro-scientific Findings:

Neuro-scientific investigations have shed light on the mechanisms underlying the positive effects of mindfulness on depression. Studies using brain imaging techniques have shown that regular mindfulness practice can lead to structural and functional changes in the brain. For example, mindfulness has been associated with increased activity in areas of the brain involved in emotion regulation, such as the prefrontal cortex, and decreased activity in regions linked to rumination and self-referential thinking, such as the default mode network. These changes suggest that mindfulness can reshape neural circuits related to emotional processing and self-awareness, contributing to its therapeutic effects on depression.

Section 4: Establishing Intention and Commitment to a Meditation Practice

Setting Clear Intentions:

To embark on a mindful meditation journey, it is crucial to

establish clear intentions. Take some time to reflect on why you want to cultivate mindfulness, what goals you wish to achieve, and how it can contribute to your healing process. Setting clear intentions provides a compass for your practice and helps you stay focused and motivated.

Building Consistency and Commitment:

Consistency is key in reaping the benefits of mindful meditation. Start small by dedicating a few minutes each day to practice. Gradually increase the duration as you build a habit. Create a dedicated space for your meditation practice, free from distractions, where you can cultivate a sense of calm and tranquility. Set a regular schedule that works for you and commit to showing up for your practice, even on days when it feels challenging. Remember that the benefits of meditation often emerge through consistent effort and dedication.

Overcoming Challenges:

Like any new endeavor, mindful meditation may come with challenges. It's important to anticipate and address these obstacles to maintain a consistent practice. Common challenges include finding time in a busy schedule, dealing with distractions, and navigating resistance or impatience. Consider integrating mindfulness into your daily routine by finding pockets of time that work for you, such as early mornings or before bedtime. Minimize distractions by turning off notifications on your electronic devices and creating a peaceful environment. When faced with
resistance or impatience, remind yourself of the long-term benefits of mindfulness and approach yourself with kindness and patience. Remember that meditation is a practice, and each moment is an opportunity for growth and learning.

Cultivating Self-Compassion:

Throughout your meditation journey, it is vital to approach yourself with self-compassion. Be gentle and understanding with yourself, accepting that meditation is a process that unfolds gradually. Embrace both the joys and difficulties you encounter

along the way, knowing that each moment is an opportunity for growth and healing. Treat yourself with kindness and compassion, cultivating a nurturing and supportive inner dialogue. Remember that self-compassion is an integral part of the mindfulness journey, allowing you to develop a deeper sense of self-acceptance and well-being.

Conclusion:

In this chapter, we explored the foundations of mindful meditation. We introduced the concept of mindfulness and its benefits for mental health, delved into the origins and principles of mindful meditation, and examined the scientific evidence supporting its effectiveness in addressing depression. Additionally, we emphasized the importance of establishing intention and commitment to a meditation practice, providing practical tips for building consistency, overcoming challenges, and cultivating self-compassion. With this foundation in place, you are now equipped with the knowledge and tools to embark on your journey of cultivating inner peace and healing through mindful meditation. In the subsequent chapters of this book, we will dive deeper into specific techniques and practices that will further support your path to well-being. Remember, the journey towards inner peace and healing begins with the foundations of mindfulness, and with each step, you can cultivate greater self-awareness, resilience, and joy in your life.

CHAPTER 3: GETTING STARTED WITH MINDFUL MEDITATION

Mindful meditation has proven to be a powerful tool for managing and alleviating symptoms of depression. In this chapter, we will delve into the practical aspects of getting started with mindful meditation. We will explore how to create a conducive meditation environment, cultivate a beginner's mind, overcome common misconceptions, and discover different meditation techniques suitable for individuals dealing with depression. Additionally, we will discuss setting realistic expectations and developing a regular meditation routine to maximize the benefits of this practice.

Section 1: Creating a Conducive Meditation Environment

To fully immerse yourself in the practice of mindful meditation, it is essential to create a calm and supportive environment. Here are some key considerations:

Finding a Quiet Space:

Select a quiet and comfortable space where you can meditate without distractions. It could be a designated room, a cozy corner, or any area where you feel at ease. Ensure that the space is free from clutter and has a calming ambiance.

Eliminating Distractions:

Minimize external stimuli by turning off electronic devices, choosing a time when interruptions are unlikely, and informing others of your meditation schedule. Consider using earplugs or an eye mask if necessary to block out noise or light.

Creating Ambiance:

Enhance the atmosphere with soft lighting, pleasant scents, and soothing background music or nature sounds if preferred. Experiment with what promotes a sense of tranquility for you. Some people find lighting candles or using essential oils helpful in creating a serene environment.

Comfortable Seating:

Choose a chair, cushion, or meditation bench that provides adequate support and allows you to maintain an upright posture. The goal is to find a comfortable position that keeps you alert and relaxed, without inducing strain or discomfort.

Section 2: Cultivating a Beginner's Mind and Overcoming Common Misconceptions

When starting your mindful meditation journey, it is important to adopt a beginner's mind and let go of preconceived notions.

Here's how:

Embracing Curiosity:

Approach meditation with an open and curious mindset, leaving behind expectations and judgments. Be receptive to each experience as it unfolds, without striving for a particular outcome. Embrace the present moment with a sense of wonder and exploration.

Letting Go of Misconceptions:

Address common misconceptions about meditation, such as the need to clear the mind completely or the belief that it will instantly solve all problems. Understand that meditation is a process that unfolds over time. It is not about achieving a state of complete thoughtlessness but rather cultivating a non-judgmental awareness of your thoughts and emotions.

Embracing Imperfection:

Release the pressure of achieving perfection in your meditation practice. Accept that thoughts and distractions will arise, and it is part of the human experience. The key is to notice these distractions without getting caught up in them, and gently guide your attention back to the present moment. Be kind to yourself and cultivate self-compassion throughout your meditation journey.

Section 3: Exploring Different Meditation Techniques Suitable for Depression

There are various meditation techniques that can be beneficial for individuals struggling with depression. Here are a few techniques to explore:

Breath Awareness:

Focus your attention on the natural rhythm of your breath. Observe the inhalation and exhalation without judgment, using the breath as an anchor to the present moment. Whenever your mind wanders, gently bring your attention back to the breath. This technique helps cultivate a sense of calm and centeredness while enhancing your ability to observe thoughts and emotions without getting caught up in them.

Body Scan:

Bring awareness to different parts of your body, systematically scanning from head to toe. Notice any sensations, tensions, or areas of discomfort without trying to change them. This technique promotes a deeper connection with your body and helps you develop an attitude of acceptance and self-care.

Loving-Kindness Meditation:

Cultivate feelings of love, compassion, and kindness towards yourself and others. Begin by directing loving-kindness towards yourself, repeating phrases such as "May I be happy, may I be healthy, may I live with ease."

Gradually extend these wishes to loved ones, neutral

individuals, and even challenging individuals. This practice nurtures positive emotions and fosters a sense of interconnectedness and empathy.

Guided Meditations:

Utilize guided meditations specifically designed for individuals with depression. These recordings or apps provide step-by-step instructions, soothing guidance, and support throughout the meditation process. Guided meditations can be particularly helpful for beginners or those who prefer external guidance.

Section 4: Setting Realistic Expectations and Developing a Regular Meditation Routine

To make the most of your mindful meditation practice, it is crucial to set realistic expectations and establish a consistent routine:

Realistic Expectations:

Understand that meditation is not a quick fix, and its benefits may unfold gradually. Avoid placing undue pressure on yourself and embrace the journey of self-discovery and healing. Some sessions may be more challenging than others, and that is perfectly normal. Trust in the process and be patient with yourself.

Start Small:

Begin with shorter meditation sessions, such as 5 to 10 minutes per day, and gradually increase the duration as you become more comfortable. It is better to have consistent, shorter sessions than sporadic, longer sessions. As you build your meditation practice, you can gradually extend the duration to 20 minutes or more.

Consistency is Key:

Establish a regular meditation routine by setting aside dedicated time each day for your practice. Consistency helps cultivate a habit

and allows you to experience the cumulative benefits of meditation over time. Choose a time that works best for you, whether it's in the morning, during a lunch break, or before bedtime.

Flexibility and Adaptation:

Be open to adjusting your meditation routine as needed. Life circumstances may change, and it's essential to find a balance that suits your current situation. Explore different times of the day or experiment with different techniques to find what works best for you. Remember, the goal is to integrate meditation into your life in a way that is sustainable and supportive.

Seek Support and Guidance:

Consider joining a meditation group, attending mindfulness workshops, or seeking guidance from a qualified meditation teacher or therapist. Connecting with others on a similar path can provide encouragement, accountability, and valuable insights. A teacher or therapist can offer personalized guidance, address any challenges you may encounter, and provide additional resources to support your meditation journey.

Conclusion:

In this chapter, we have explored the foundational aspects of getting started with mindful meditation for depression. Creating a conducive meditation environment, cultivating a beginner's mind, and exploring different techniques suitable for individuals with

depression are essential steps in this journey. Additionally, setting realistic expectations and developing a regular meditation routine are crucial for long-term benefits and sustained progress in your meditation practice.

Remember, each meditation session is an opportunity for self-care, growth, and healing. Embrace the process with patience, kindness, and a genuine commitment to your well-being. As you continue on your mindful meditation journey, you will discover the profound effects it can have on your mental health, providing you with inner peace, clarity, and resilience in the face of depression.

In the next chapter, we will delve deeper into the specific benefits of mindful meditation for depression and how it can positively impact your mental and emotional well-being. We will explore scientific research, personal anecdotes, and practical strategies for integrating mindful meditation into your overall treatment plan for depression.

By dedicating yourself to this practice and nurturing your inner peace, you are taking an empowering step towards healing and cultivating a sense of balance and harmony in your life..

CHAPTER 4: CULTIVATING MINDFUL AWARENESS

In this chapter, we delve deep into the practice of cultivating mindful awareness, a powerful tool for managing depression and fostering inner peace and healing. Understanding how to develop deep concentration and expand our awareness.

We will explore how to integrate mindful awareness into our daily lives. The true benefits of mindfulness are experienced when we bring the practice off the meditation cushion and into our everyday activities. By cultivating mindfulness in our daily routines, we can enhance our overall well-being and bring greater peace and harmony into our lives.

Section 1: Deepening Concentration and Focus through Mindfulness of Breath

In this section, we delve into the practice of using the breath as a focal point for mindfulness meditation. The breath serves as an anchor to the present moment, allowing us to cultivate concentration and deepen our focus. Through consistent practice, we can develop a greater sense of calm and stability within ourselves.

Exercise: Breath Awareness Meditation

1. Find a quiet and comfortable place to sit. Sit in an upright position, with your spine straight but not rigid.

2. Close your eyes gently and bring your attention to your breath. Observe the natural flow of your breath, without trying to control or change it.

3. Notice the sensation of the breath as it enters and leaves your nostrils. Pay attention to the temperature, texture, and rhythm of each breath.

4. If your mind wanders, gently guide your attention back to the breath. Be patient and compassionate with yourself as you do this, as it is normal for the mind to wander.

5. As you continue to practice, gradually extend your awareness to include the entire breath cycle, from the moment it enters your body to the moment it leaves.

6. Allow yourself to be fully present with each breath, letting go of any distractions or worries that arise. Simply observe and experience the breath as it is.

Through the practice of breath awareness meditation, we develop the ability to anchor our attention in the present moment.

consciously focusing on the breath, we cultivate a sense of centeredness and stability within ourselves. This practice helps to calm the mind, reduce anxiety, and enhance our ability to concentrate.

Section 2: Expanding Awareness to Include Bodily Sensations, Emotions, and Thoughts

In this section, we explore the practice of expanding mindfulness to include the various sensations, emotions, and thoughts that arise within us. By cultivating a non-judgmental and curious attitude, we can develop a deeper understanding of our inner experiences and their connection to our emotional well-being.

Exercise: Body Scan Meditation

1. Find a comfortable lying-down position, either on a yoga mat or a soft surface. Close your eyes gently and bring your attention to your body.

2. Begin by directing your focus to your toes. Notice any sensations, such as warmth, tingling, or tension. Allow yourself to fully experience these sensations without judgment or analysis.

3. Slowly move your attention up through your feet, calves, knees, thighs, and so on, scanning your entire body. Take your time with each area, observing any physical sensations

that arise.

4. As you encounter areas of tension or discomfort, practice sending your breath to those areas. Imagine the breath

flowing in and out, bringing relaxation and release.

5. If your mind becomes distracted by thoughts or emotions, gently guide your attention back to the physical sensations of your body. Use the breath as an anchor to keep you grounded in the present moment.

By practicing the body scan meditation, we develop a deep connection with our physical bodies. This practice cultivates body awareness and helps us to recognize any areas of tension or discomfort. By directing our breath and attention to these areas, we can promote relaxation and release. This practice also fosters a sense of embodiment, grounding us in the present moment and enhancing our overall well-being.

Section 3: Developing the Skill of Observing without Judgment or Attachment

In this section, we focus on cultivating the ability to observe our thoughts, emotions, and sensations without judgment or attachment. By developing a sense of detachment from our inner experiences, we can create space for self-reflection, insight, and emotional healing.

Exercise: Thoughts and Emotions Meditation

1. Find a comfortable seated position and close your eyes gently. Take a few deep breaths to settle into the present moment.

2. Allow your thoughts and emotions to arise naturally, without trying to suppress or control them. Observe them as if you were an impartial observer, watching clouds passing by in the sky.

3. Notice any judgments or attachments that arise in response to your thoughts and emotions. Practice letting go of these judgments or attachments, reminding yourself that they are transient and not a true reflection of your self-worth.

4. As thoughts or emotions arise, label them without getting caught up in their content. For example, if a thought about the past arises, simply note it as "thinking" and return to observing without further engagement.

5. Remember to approach this practice with kindness and compassion toward yourself. It is natural for the mind to wander or for challenging emotions to arise. Treat yourself with understanding and acceptance throughout the process.

By practicing thoughts and emotions meditation, we develop the skill of observing our inner experiences without getting entangled in their stories or judgments. This practice allows us to cultivate a sense of spaciousness and freedom from the grip of our thoughts and emotions. As we observe our thoughts and emotions with non-judgmental awareness, we gain insight into their impermanent nature and begin to develop a healthier relationship with our inner world.

Section 4: Cultivating a Compassionate and Accepting Attitude towards Oneself

In this section, we explore the transformative power of self-compassion and acceptance. By cultivating a gentle and loving attitude towards ourselves, we can foster healing and inner peace.

Exercise: Loving-Kindness Meditation

1. Find a comfortable posture, either seated or lying down, and close your eyes gently. Take a few moments to settle into

   your body and connect with your breath.

2. Begin by directing loving-kindness towards yourself. Repeat silently or out loud the following phrases, allowing their meaning to resonate within you: "May I be happy. May I be healthy. May I be safe. May I live with ease."

3. As you recite these phrases, imagine sending warmth and kindness to every part of your being. Visualize yourself surrounded by a soft, radiant light of love and compassion.

4. If distractions arise, such as self-critical thoughts or judgments, acknowledge them without judgment and gently return your focus to the loving-kindness phrases.

5. After a few minutes, expand your loving-kindness outward,

6. directing it towards others. Begin with someone you deeply care about, then gradually include neutral individuals and even those with whom you have difficulties. Repeat the same phrases, adjusting them to address the specific person.

7. Finally, extend loving-kindness to all beings, recognizing our interconnectedness and common humanity. Wish for the happiness, health, safety, and ease of all sentient beings.

By practicing loving-kindness meditation, we cultivate a compassionate and accepting attitude towards ourselves and others.

This practice nurtures self-love, self-acceptance, and a sense of interconnectedness with all beings. Through the power of loving-kindness, we can heal our wounds, dissolve self-criticism, and cultivate a deep sense of inner peace and well-being.

Section 5: Integrating Mindful Awareness into Daily Life

Exercise: Mindful Daily Activities

1. Choose a daily activity that you engage in regularly, such as brushing your teeth, taking a shower, or eating a meal.

2. Before you begin the activity, take a moment to pause and ground yourself in the present moment. Take a few deep breaths and bring your attention to your body and senses.

3. As you engage in the activity, bring your full attention to each moment. Notice the sensations, smells, tastes, and textures associated with the activity. Be fully present with the experience without rushing or multitasking.

4. If your mind starts to wander or if you become distracted, gently guide your attention back to the present moment and the activity at hand. Use the breath as an anchor to bring you back to the present.

5. Approach the activity with a sense of curiosity and non-judgment. Notice any thoughts or judgments that arise, and practice letting them go without getting caught up in them.

By practicing mindfulness in our daily activities, we can

transform routine tasks into opportunities for presence and awareness. This practice helps us break free from autopilot mode and connect more deeply with the richness of each moment.

Conclusion:

In this chapter, we have explored the cultivation of mindful awareness as a powerful tool for healing and inner peace. By

deepening our concentration and focus through mindfulness of breath, expanding our awareness to include bodily sensations, emotions, and thoughts, developing the skill of observing without judgment or attachment, and cultivating a compassionate and accepting attitude towards ourselves, we lay the foundation for a transformative and healing mindfulness practice.

Remember that mindfulness is a journey, and it takes time and practice to cultivate these qualities. Be patient and gentle with yourself as you explore the exercises and integrate mindful awareness into your daily life. Allow yourself to experience the benefits of mindfulness at your own pace, knowing that every moment of mindful awareness brings you closer to cultivating inner peace and healing.

May your journey of cultivating mindful awareness be filled with self-discovery, compassion, and profound transformation.

CHAPTER 5: WORKING WITH DIFFICULT EMOTIONS

In this chapter, we will explore the profound connection between thoughts, emotions, and depression. We will examine the role of thoughts in shaping emotions and how they contribute to depressive states. Additionally, we will delve into techniques rooted in mindfulness to navigate and transform challenging emotions. We will emphasize the importance of cultivating self-compassion and self-care as essential components of emotional well-being. Finally, we will address resistance and provide guidance for overcoming obstacles that may arise during the meditation practice.

Section 1: Understanding the Connection between Thoughts, Emotions, and Depression

Our thoughts have a significant influence on our emotional well-being. Negative thought patterns often contribute to the development and deepening of depression. These thoughts create a feedback loop, where negative emotions reinforce negative thoughts, and vice versa. By understanding this connection, we can begin to disrupt this cycle and cultivate a healthier mindset.

Exploring the relationship between thoughts, emotions, and depression allows us to recognize the power of thoughts in shaping our experiences. We can learn to identify negative thought patterns, such as self-criticism, rumination, and catastrophizing, which contribute to depressive episodes. By becoming aware of these patterns, we can start challenging and transforming

them.

Exercise 1: Thought Observation
Instructions:

1. Set aside a few minutes each day for this exercise.

2. Sit in a comfortable position, close your eyes, and take a few deep breaths to center yourself.

3. Observe your thoughts without judgment or attachment.

4. Notice any negative or self-critical thoughts that arise.

5. Label these thoughts as "thinking" and gently redirect your attention back to the present moment.

6. Repeat this process of observing and redirecting whenever negative thoughts arise.

Section 2: Techniques for Navigating and Transforming Challenging Emotions

Mindfulness provides powerful tools for navigating and transforming difficult emotions. By cultivating mindful awareness, we can develop a non-judgmental and accepting attitude towards our emotions. Instead of suppressing or avoiding them, we learn to observe them with curiosity and compassion.

One effective technique for working with difficult emotions is the RAIN technique: Recognize, Accept, Investigate, and Nurture. This four-step process involves recognizing the emotions that arise, accepting them without resistance or judgment, investigating their underlying causes and beliefs, and nurturing oneself with compassion and self-care. The RAIN technique empowers us to engage with our emotions mindfully, allowing us to transform them with kindness and understanding.

Breath awareness meditation is another valuable practice for navigating challenging emotions. By using the breath as an anchor, we can cultivate stability and regulate our emotions. Focused breathing techniques help calm and soothe the mind, allowing us to observe and transform emotional energy.

Exercise 2: RAIN Technique
Instructions:

1. Find a quiet and comfortable space to practice this exercise.

2. Close your eyes, take a few deep breaths, and bring your attention to your emotions.

3. Recognize the emotions that are present in this moment. Label them without judgment.

4. Accept the emotions without trying to change or fix them. Allow them to be as they are.

5. .Investigate the underlying causes and beliefs associated with these emotions. Ask yourself what thoughts or experiences may have triggered them.

6. Nurture yourself with self-compassion and self-care. Offer yourself kind and supportive words. Engage in an activity that brings you joy or soothes your emotions.

7. Take a few moments to reflect on the experience and notice any shifts or insights that arise.

Section 3: Cultivating Self-Compassion and Self-Care

Self-compassion is a vital component of emotional well-being.

By treating ourselves with kindness and understanding, we can alleviate suffering and foster healing. Developing self-compassion practices, such as self-compassionate self-talk, self-compassion meditations, and self-compassionate acts, helps us cultivate a nurturing and supportive inner relationship.

In addition to self-compassion, self-care plays a significant role in managing difficult emotions. Recognizing the importance of self-care allows us to prioritize activities and practices that nourish our emotional well-being. This may include engaging in hobbies, spending time in nature, practicing relaxation techniques, seeking social support, or engaging in physical exercise. By integrating self-care into our daily lives, we create a foundation for emotional resilience and balance.

Exercise 3: Breath Awareness Meditation
Instructions:

1. Find a quiet and comfortable space where you won't be disturbed.

2. Sit in a relaxed position, either on a cushion or a chair, with your back straight and your hands resting comfortably.

3. Close your eyes and bring your attention to your breath.

4. Notice the sensation of the breath as it enters and leaves your body.

5. If your mind wanders, gently bring your focus back to the breath without judgment.

6. As you continue to breathe, observe any emotions that arise without becoming attached to them.

8. Allow the breath to be a source of stability and calm as you

navigate and transform your emotions.

Section 4: Addressing Resistance and Overcoming Obstacles

Resistance is a common challenge in meditation practice, especially when working with difficult emotions. We may resist experiencing and exploring certain emotions due to fear, discomfort, or ingrained patterns. Recognizing resistance is the first step toward overcoming it.

Developing self-awareness is essential in identifying personal challenges and barriers that arise during the meditation practice. By cultivating mindfulness, we can observe our resistance without judgment or self-criticism. This awareness empowers us to investigate the underlying reasons for resistance and develop strategies to overcome it.

To overcome obstacles in the meditation practice, patience and persistence are key. Working with difficult emotions requires time and dedication. It's important to cultivate patience with ourselves, allowing emotions to arise and pass without trying to force them away. By acknowledging that healing and transformation take time, we can approach our practice with a sense of gentleness and understanding.

Developing resilience is also crucial in navigating obstacles. There may be times when our progress feels slow or when we encounter setbacks. During these moments, it's essential to cultivate resilience and remain committed to the practice. Remind yourself of the benefits you have experienced thus far and trust in the process of emotional healing.

Seeking support from a trusted teacher, mentor, or therapist can provide guidance and encouragement when facing obstacles. They can offer insights, techniques, and personalized strategies to help

you overcome challenges and deepen your practice.

Exercise 4: Self-Compassion Practice
Instructions:

1. Find a quiet and comfortable space where you can sit or lie down.

2. Take a few deep breaths to relax your body and mind.

3.Bring to mind a difficult emotion or experience that you are currently facing.

4. Offer yourself words of compassion and understanding. Say these words silently or out loud, addressing yourself directly.

5. Imagine extending warmth and kindness towards yourself, embracing your emotions with compassion.

6. Repeat affirmations or phrases such as "May I be gentle with myself," "May I find peace and healing," or "May I be kind and compassionate towards myself."

7. Take a few moments to rest in this self-compassionate space and observe any shifts in your emotional well-being.

In conclusion, working with difficult emotions is an integral part of mindful meditation for depression. By understanding the connection between thoughts, emotions, and depression, exploring techniques to navigate and transform challenging emotions, cultivating self-compassion and self-care, and addressing resistance and overcoming obstacles, you can cultivate inner peace and healing. Remember, this journey requires patience, persistence, and self-compassion. With dedication and a mindful approach, you can develop the skills to transform difficult emotions and find emotional

well-being. My hopes are that you don't find the exercises redundant and realize they are getting deeper as we progress. They are to ease you into the progression. This is integral for finding peace and freedom from depression.

CHAPTER 6: MINDFULNESS IN DAILY LIFE

In this chapter, we will explore the practical aspects of incorporating mindfulness into your daily life. By integrating mindfulness into your everyday activities and routines, you can develop a greater sense of inner peace and healing. We will discuss how to apply mindfulness to manage stress, anxiety, and negative thinking patterns. Additionally, we will explore how mindfulness can enhance your relationships and communication skills. Lastly, we will delve into using mindfulness to cultivate self-awareness and self-regulation.

Section 1: Integrating Mindfulness into Everyday Activities and Routines

Mindful Eating:

Mindful eating involves bringing awareness to the process of eating, which can help you develop a healthier relationship with food and cultivate a sense of gratitude for nourishment. To practice mindful eating, follow these steps:

- Before you start eating, take a moment to observe the appearance, smell, and texture of your food. Pay attention to any sensations or cravings that arise.

- As you take each bite, chew slowly and savor the flavors and textures. Notice the sensations in your mouth and how the food feels as you swallow.

- Avoid distractions such as TV, phones, or reading while eating. Instead, focus your attention on the act of eating and the nourishment it provides.

- Pay attention to your body's hunger and fullness cues. Eat until you feel satisfied, rather than eating mindlessly or until you're overly full.

- Practice gratitude for the food you consume. Reflect on the effort and resources that went into producing the meal and express appreciation for the nourishment it provides.

Mindful Walking:

Mindful walking is a practice that involves bringing awareness to the act of walking, allowing you to be fully present in the moment. Follow these steps to practice mindful walking:

- Begin by finding a quiet and safe space to walk, either indoors or outdoors.

- As you start walking, bring your attention to the physical sensations in your feet and legs. Notice the contact between your feet and the ground.

- Pay attention to the movement of your body as you take each step. Observe the shifting of your weight, the swinging of your arms, and the rhythm of your breath.

- Engage your senses by noticing the sights, sounds, and smells around you. Allow yourself to be fully present in you environment without judgment.

- If your mind wanders, gently bring your focus back to the sensations of walking and the present moment.

Mindful Daily Rituals:

Daily rituals offer an opportunity to infuse mindfulness into your routine activities. Here are some suggestions for incorporating mindfulness into various daily rituals:

- Morning Routine: Begin your day with a few moments of mindful breathing or a short meditation. Bring awareness to each step of your morning routine, such as brushing your teeth or preparing breakfast.

- Household Chores: Approach household chores mindfully by paying attention to the sensations and movements involved. Engage your senses in activities like washing dishes or folding laundry.

- Bedtime Routine: Create a mindful bedtime routine by dimming the lights, practicing relaxation exercises, and reflecting on your day with gratitude. Slow down and savor the process of getting ready for bed.

- Transitions: Use transitions between activities as opportunities for mindfulness. Slow down and take a few deep breaths before moving from one task to another. Bring your attention to the present moment and let go of any lingering thoughts or stresses from the previous activity.

Section 2: Applying Mindfulness to Manage Stress, Anxiety, and Negative Thinking Patterns

Mindful Breathing:

Mindful breathing is a powerful tool for managing stress and anxiety. It brings your focus to the present moment and helps calm your mind. Try the following exercise:

- Find a quiet and comfortable place to sit or lie down.

- Close your eyes and take a few deep breaths, allowing your body to relax.

- Shift your attention to your breath. Notice the sensation of air entering and leaving your body.

- Take slow, deep breaths, counting to four as you inhale and counting to four as you exhale.

- As thoughts or distractions arise, acknowledge them without judgment and gently guide your focus back to your breath.

- Practice this exercise for a few minutes each day, gradually increasing the duration as you become more comfortable.

Mindful Body Scan:

The mindful body scan is a practice that helps you deepen your awareness of bodily sensations and release tension. Follow these steps:

- Find a comfortable position, either lying down or sitting with your spine straight.

- Close your eyes and bring your attention to your body.

  Begin at the top of your head and slowly scan down through your body, paying attention to any sensations or areas of tension.

- As you encounter areas of tension, consciously relax those muscles and breathe into the sensations.

- Continue scanning your body, moving down to your neck, shoulders, arms, chest, abdomen, hips, legs, and feet.

- Take your time and allow yourself to fully experience the sensations without judgment or the need to change anything.

- After completing the body scan, take a few moments to rest in a state of relaxed awareness.

Mindful Journaling:

Mindful journaling is a reflective practice that helps you become aware of your thoughts and emotions, offering insights into negative thinking patterns. Follow these guidelines:

- Set aside dedicated time for journaling in a quiet and comfortable space.

- Begin by writing freely without judgment or self-editing. Let your thoughts flow onto the paper.

- Pay attention to any recurring negative thoughts or patterns that arise. Notice the emotions associated with them.

- Challenge negative thoughts by questioning their validity and

- exploring alternative perspectives.
-
- Cultivate self-compassion by writing down positive affirmations or engaging in self-appreciation exercises.

- End each journaling session by expressing gratitude for the opportunity to explore your inner world.

Section 3: Bringing Mindfulness into Relationships and Communication

Mindful Listening:

Mindful listening is a practice that allows you to be fully present when others are speaking, fostering deeper connection and understanding. Try the following exercises:

- Choose a partner or a friend and engage in a conversation.

- Focus your attention on the speaker, maintaining eye contact and giving them your full presence.

- Resist the urge to interrupt or formulate a response while the other person is speaking.

- Practice active listening by nodding, using affirming

gestures, and providing verbal cues to show that you are engaged.

- Reflect back on what the speaker has said to ensure understanding and to validate their experience.

- Notice any judgments or assumptions that arise and let them go, returning to a state of open curiosity and receptivity.

- After the conversation, take a moment to reflection the experience. Notice how mindful listening affected your connection with the other person and your understanding of their perspective.

Mindful Speaking:

Mindful speaking involves choosing your words consciously and
speaking with kindness and compassion. Practice the following exercises:

- Before speaking, take a moment to pause and connect with your breath. This helps you become present and aware of your intentions.

- Consider the impact of your words on others. Ask yourself if your words are necessary, true, and helpful.

- Speak with kindness and compassion, using a gentle tone and avoiding harsh or judgmental language.

- Take note of your body language and non-verbal cues, ensuring they align with your words and convey openness and respect.

- Practice active self-awareness while speaking, noticing any tendencies to dominate the conversation or speak impulsively.

- If you catch yourself straying from mindful speaking, pause,

-

-

- take a breath, and course-correct, choosing words that align with your intentions.

-

Mindful Conflict Resolution:

Mindful conflict resolution involves bringing mindfulness to moments of disagreement or tension, fostering understanding and compassion. Follow these steps:

- Before engaging in a conflict, take a few moments to ground yourself through mindful breathing. This helps you approach the situation with clarity and calmness.

- Practice active listening by giving the other person your full attention and allowing them to express their perspective without interruption.

- Cultivate empathy by putting yourself in the other person's shoes and seeking to understand their underlying needs and emotions.

- Respond mindfully, choosing your words carefully and avoiding reactive or defensive responses.

- Look for common ground and areas of agreement, focusing on solutions rather than dwelling on differences.

- Take breaks when needed, allowing both parties to regroup and reflect before continuing the conversation.

- Remember that conflict resolution takes time and patience. Approach the process with an open mind and a willingness to find a mutually beneficial resolution.

Section 4: Using Mindfulness to Enhance Self-Awareness and Self-Regulation

Mindful Self-Reflection:

Mindful self-reflection is a practice that allows you to gain insight into your thoughts, emotions, and behaviors. Try the following exercises:

- Set aside dedicated time for self-reflection in a quiet and comfortable space.

- Begin by bringing your attention to your breath, grounding yourself in the present moment.

- Reflect on your thoughts, emotions, and reactions to various situations throughout the day. Notice any patterns or triggers.

- Cultivate self-awareness without judgment, allowing yourself to observe your experiences with curiosity and compassion.

- Set intentions for personal growth and development based on your reflections, identifying areas where you would like to make positive changes.

- Consider keeping a self-reflection journal to document your insights, progress, and intentions.

Mindful Emotion Regulation:

Mindful emotion regulation involves developing the ability to recognize and regulate your emotions in a healthy and constructive manner. Practice the following exercises:

- When you notice the presence of an emotion, take a moment to pause and acknowledge it without judgment.

- Bring your attention to the physical sensations associated with the emotion, such as tightness in the chest or a knot in

- the stomach.

- Take slow, deep breaths to calm your nervous system, allowing yourself to observe the emotion without being overwhelmed by it.

- Engage in self-compassion by offering kind and supportive words to yourself, acknowledging that it is normal to experience a range of emotions.

- Label the emotion you are experiencing, recognizing that emotions are temporary and will pass.

- Explore the underlying causes or triggers of the emotion, considering any unmet needs or unaddressed concerns.

- Choose a healthy and appropriate way to respond to the emotion. This may involve seeking support from others, engaging in self-care activities, or practicing relaxation techniques.

- Regularly practice mindfulness meditation or other mindfulness exercises to strengthen your ability to regulate emotions and cultivate emotional balance.

Conclusion:

Incorporating mindfulness into your daily life can have profound effects on managing stress, anxiety, and negative thinking patterns. By integrating mindfulness into your activities, relationships, and self-reflection, you can cultivate a greater sense of inner peace,
healing, and self-awareness. Remember that mindfulness is a practice, and it takes time and consistency to develop. With dedication and patience, you can make mindfulness an integral part of your life, leading to a more mindful and fulfilling existence.

CHAPTER 7: MINDFUL MOVEMENT AND BODY AWARENESS

In Chapter 7, we will explore the powerful benefits of incorporating mindful movement practices into our journey of healing from depression. By engaging in activities such as yoga, Tai Chi, and walking meditation, we can tap into the transformative potential of the mind-body connection. Through these exercises, we will cultivate body awareness, release tension, and promote deep relaxation, ultimately integrating mindful movement into our overall mindfulness practice.

Section 1: Exploring the Benefits of Mindful Movement Practices

The Mind-Body Connection:

Engaging in mindful movement practices allows us to bridge the gap between our minds and bodies. By recognizing the interconnectedness of our physical and mental well-being, we can harness movement as a powerful tool for managing depression. Take a moment to reflect on the following questions:

- How does movement affect your mood and mental state?

- Can you recall a time when engaging in physical activity had a positive impact on your well-being?

Yoga as Mindful Movement:

Yoga is a wonderful practice for cultivating mindfulness and body awareness. Here is a simple yoga exercise for you to try:

- Find a quiet space and come to a comfortable seated position.

- Close your eyes and take a few deep breaths, allowing your body to relax.

- Begin to gently move your body, stretching and awakening each muscle group.

- Pay attention to the physical sensations that arise as you move. Notice the subtle shifts in energy and tension.

- Focus on your breath, allowing it to guide your movements.

- Engage in this mindful yoga practice for at least 10 minutes, being fully present with each movement and breath.

Tai Chi for Mindful Movement:

Tai Chi combines graceful, flowing movements with mindful awareness. Try this basic Tai Chi exercise to experience its benefits:

- Stand with your feet shoulder-width apart, knees slightly bent.

- Relax your arms by your sides and let them hang naturally.

-   Shift your weight to your left foot as you raise your right foot slightly off the ground.

-   Slowly move your right foot forward, heel touching the ground first, followed by the ball of your foot. Shift your weight to your right foot as you bring your left foot forward in the same manner.

-   Continue this slow, deliberate movement, coordinating it with your breath.

-   Pay attention to the sensations in your feet, legs, and the rest of your body as you move mindfully.

Walking Meditation:

Walking meditation allows us to bring mindfulness into our daily
activities. Follow these steps for a walking meditation practice:

-   Find a quiet and safe space to walk, preferably outdoors.

-   Begin by standing still, grounding yourself, and taking a few deep breaths.

-   Start walking slowly, paying attention to the sensation of each step touching the ground.

-   Focus your attention on the physical sensations in your feet and legs as you move forward.

-   Notice the rhythmic movement of your body and the changing scenery around you.

- If your mind wanders, gently bring your attention back to the physical sensations of walking.

- Engage in this walking meditation for at least 10 minutes, allowing yourself to fully immerse in the experience.

Section 2: Cultivating Body Awareness and Reconnecting with Physical Sensations

The Importance of Body Awareness:

Body awareness is a fundamental aspect of mindfulness and plays a crucial role in managing depression. By cultivating body awareness, we can reconnect with our physical sensations and develop a deeper understanding of ourselves. Here is an exercise to help you enhance your body awareness:

- Find a comfortable seated position or lie down in a relaxed position.

- Close your eyes and take a few deep breaths to settle into the present moment.

- Begin to scan your body from head to toe, noticing any areas of tension, discomfort, or ease.

- As you scan, bring gentle attention to each body part, starting with your head and face, moving down to your neck, shoulders, arms, chest, back, abdomen, hips, legs, and feet.

- Acknowledge any physical sensations you encounter, whether they are pleasant, neutral, or uncomfortable.

- Avoid judging or trying to change the sensations; simply observe them with curiosity and acceptance.

- Spend a few moments on each body part, allowing yourself

- to fully experience the sensations present.

- Gradually expand your awareness to encompass your entire body as a unified whole.

- Throughout the day, practice periodically checking in with your body and noticing any tension or sensations that arise.

Breath and Body Awareness:

The breath serves as an anchor to the present moment and can deepen our body awareness. Try this breath and body awareness exercise:

- Find a comfortable seated position with your spine straight and shoulders relaxed.

- Take a few deep breaths, allowing your body to settle and relax.

- Direct your attention to your breath, noticing the sensation of the inhale and exhale.

- As you continue to breathe, bring your awareness to the physical sensations of the breath in your body.

- Notice the rising and falling of your abdomen or the sensation of air flowing in and out through your nose.

- Expand your awareness to include the subtle movements and sensations in different parts of your body as you breathe.

- If your mind wanders, gently guide your attention back to the breath and the physical sensations.

Practice this breath and body awareness exercise for a few minutes each day, gradually increasing the duration as you become more comfortable.

Section 3: Utilizing Mindful Movement to Release Tension and Promote Relaxation

Releasing Tension through Mindful Movement:

Mindful movement practices offer a powerful way to release physical and emotional tension. Try this exercise to release tension in your body:

- Stand with your feet hip-width apart and relax your arms by your sides.

- Take a deep breath in, and as you exhale, gently roll your shoulders back and down, releasing any tension held in that area.

- Inhale deeply again, and as you exhale, allow your head and neck to relax, releasing any tightness or stiffness.

- Continue this process, moving through your body and consciously releasing tension from your jaw, chest, arms, abdomen, hips, legs, and feet.

- As you release tension, imagine it melting away, leaving

your body feeling lighter and more relaxed.

- Take a few moments to stand still and notice the sensations in your body after releasing tension.

-

- Practice this exercise regularly, especially during times when you feel particularly tense or stressed.

Relaxation Techniques in Mindful Movement:

Combining relaxation techniques with mindful movement can amplify their effects. Here's an exercise that integrates relaxation into a mindful movement practice:

- Choose a mindful movement practice that resonates with you, such as yoga, Tai Chi, or walking meditation.

- Before you begin, take a few moments to set an intention for relaxation and stress reduction during your practice.

- Start engaging in your chosen mindful movement practice, focusing on slow and deliberate movements.

- As you move, consciously relax your muscles and let go of any tension or tightness.

- With each movement, synchronize it with your breath, allowing it to guide the pace and flow of your practice.

- Pay attention to the physical sensations that arise as you move, noticing any areas of tension or discomfort.

- Whenever you encounter tension or tightness, intentionally relax those muscles and let go of the tension.

- As you continue your practice, maintain a gentle and compassionate awareness of your body and its needs.

- Towards the end of your practice, gradually slow down your movements and transition into a period of stillness.

- Take a few moments to lie down in a comfortable position and engage in a relaxation technique such as progressive muscle relaxation or deep breathing.

- Allow your body and mind to fully unwind, releasing any remaining tension and promoting a state of deep relaxation.

- When you're ready, slowly and mindfully transition back to a seated position, bringing your practice to a close.

Section 4: Incorporating Mindful Movement into an Overall

Mindfulness Practice for Depression

Creating a Mindful Movement Routine:

To incorporate mindful movement into your overall mindfulness practice, consider creating a routine that works for you. Here are some steps to help you get started:

- Reflect on your schedule and identify specific times during the week when you can dedicate to mindful movement.

- Choose one or more mindful movement practices that resonate with you, such as yoga, Tai Chi, or walking meditation.

- Set realistic goals for the frequency and duration of your mindful movement sessions, considering your current physical abilities and time constraints.

- Create a dedicated space for your ispractice, whether it's a corner of a room or an outdoor area that inspires tranquility.

- Use reminders or alarms to help you stay consistent with your mindful movement routine.

- Be flexible and open to adjusting your routine as needed to accommodate any changes or challenges that may arise.

Integrating Mindful Movement with Meditation:

Combining seated mindfulness meditation with mindful movement practices can offer a harmonious blend of stillness and movement. Here are some suggestions for integrating the two:

- Begin your practice with a few minutes of seated mindfulness meditation, focusing on your breath and cultivating present-moment awareness.

- Transition into your chosen mindful movement practice, carrying the qualities of mindfulness and body awareness with you.

- Throughout your mindful movement practice, periodically pause and bring your attention to the sensations in your body and the quality of your breath.

- After your mindful movement session, return to a seated position and engage in a period of seated meditation to further deepen your mindfulness practice.

- Use this time to reflect on the experience of mindful movement, observing any shifts in your mental and emotional state.

Conclusion:

Through the incorporation of mindful movement practices into our lives, we can cultivate body awareness, release tension, and promote deep relaxation. By integrating these practices into our overall mindfulness practice for depression, we can unlock a profound sense of inner peace and healing. Remember to approach

these exercises with patience, self-compassion, and a willingness
to explore the transformative potential of mindful movement.

CHAPTER 8: NURTURING RESILIENCE AND WELL BEING

As we come to the final chapter of "Mindful Meditation for Depression: Cultivating Inner Peace and Healing," we embark on a journey of nurturing resilience and well-being. Throughout this book, we have explored the transformative power of mindfulness and meditation in alleviating depression. Now, we shift our focus to the practices and strategies that can help you build resilience, counterbalance depressive tendencies, develop a support system, and create a holistic self-care plan. By incorporating these elements into your life, you will be better equipped to sustain your progress and embrace a more joyful and fulfilling existence.

Building Resilience through Mindfulness and Meditation:
Resilience is the ability to bounce back from adversity and maintain a sense of well-being despite life's challenges. Mindfulness and meditation serve as powerful tools for enhancing resilience. Through the practices we have explored in earlier chapters, you have learned to cultivate present-moment awareness, which allows you to develop a deeper understanding of your thoughts, emotions, and reactions. This self-awareness becomes the foundation for building resilience. By recognizing and accepting difficulties, you can respond to them with greater clarity and compassion. Regular
meditation practice strengthens your ability to remain centered and calm amidst life's ups and downs, ultimately fostering resilience.

Fostering Gratitude and Positive Emotions:

Depression often distorts our perception, making it difficult to notice
positive aspects of our lives. However, by deliberately cultivating gratitude and positive emotions, we can counterbalance this tendency and enhance our overall well-being. Mindful meditation can help you redirect your attention to the present moment and consciously acknowledge the things you appreciate. By regularly practicing gratitude, you create a positive feedback loop that uplifts your mood and cultivates a more optimistic outlook. Engaging in activities that bring you joy and consciously savoring positive experiences further enhance your emotional well-being. By nurturing gratitude and positive emotions, you can counteract depressive tendencies and experience greater resilience and contentment.

Developing a Support System and Seeking Professional Assistance:
While meditation and mindfulness can be immensely beneficial, it is crucial to recognize the importance of seeking support when needed. Developing a support system of trusted individuals, such as friends, family members, or support groups, provides a valuable network of emotional support. They can offer a listening ear, provide guidance, and remind you that you are not alone in your journey. Additionally, do not hesitate to reach out to mental health professionals who can offer specialized assistance tailored to your needs. Seeking professional help is a sign of strength and a proactive step towards healing and well-being. Therapists, counselors, or psychiatrists can provide valuable insights, tools, and interventions to complement your mindfulness and meditation practice.

Creating a Holistic Self-Care Plan:

To maintain a balanced and healthy life, it is essential,

holistic self-care plan that addresses all aspects of your well-being. Mindfulness and meditation are just one aspect of this plan. Pay attention to your overall well-being by nourishing your body, mind, and soul. A nutritious diet, regular exercise, and sufficient sleep contribute to your physical and mental vitality. Incorporate mindfulness into your daily routines, such as practicing mindful eating or engaging in mindful movement. Explore and engage in activities that bring you joy, whether it's pursuing hobbies, spending time in nature, or connecting with loved ones. Remember to prioritize self-care and make it a non-negotiable part of your life. By adopting a holistic self-care plan, you create a strong foundation for resilience and well-being.

Consider incorporating various self-care practices into your daily life. Begin by setting aside time for mindfulness and meditation practice each day. This could be in the form of a formal seated meditation, mindful walking, or even incorporating mindfulness into mundane activities such as washing dishes or
taking a shower. Allow yourself moments of stillness and presence throughout the day.

Furthermore, pay attention to your physical well-being. Ensure you are nourishing your body with a balanced and nutritious diet. Take time to engage in regular physical exercise that brings you joy and helps release tension. Whether it's yoga, running, swimming, or any other form of movement, find what resonates with you and make it a regular part of your routine.

Sleep is another crucial aspect of self-care. Make it a priority to establish a consistent sleep schedule and create a calming bedtime routine. Create a sleep-friendly environment that promotes restful sleep, such as a comfortable mattress, a dark and quiet room, and a relaxing pre-sleep ritual.

In addition to mindfulness, nutrition, exercise, and sleep, nurturing your emotional well-being is equally important. Seek out activities

that bring you joy, whether it's spending time with loved ones, engaging in hobbies, or pursuing creative outlets. Make time for laughter, playfulness, and relaxation. Engage in practices that promote self-compassion and self-acceptance.

Remember, building resilience and nurturing well-being is an ongoing process. Be patient and kind to yourself as you navigate through challenges. Regularly evaluate and adjust your self-care plan to ensure it meets your evolving needs.

Conclusion:

In conclusion, the final chapter of "Mindful Meditation for Depression: Cultivating Inner Peace and Healing" focuses on nurturing resilience and well-being. By building resilience through mindfulness and meditation, fostering gratitude and positive emotions, developing a support system, and creating a holistic self-care plan, you can enhance your overall well-being and sustain your progress on the path to healing. Embrace these practices with an open heart and commitment, knowing that they have the potential to guide you towards a more resilient, joyful, and fulfilling life. Remember, you have the strength within you to cultivate inner peace and heal from depression. May your journey be one of growth, transformation, and profound self-discovery.

CONCLUSION

In conclusion, "Mindful Meditation for Depression: Cultivating Inner Peace and Healing" has explored the transformative potential of mindful meditation as a powerful tool for individuals struggling with depression. Throughout this book, we have delved into the depths of mindfulness, uncovering its ability to bring about profound changes in our lives.

Through the practice of mindful meditation, we have witnessed how individuals can cultivate a sense of inner peace and healing. By bringing awareness to our thoughts, emotions, and sensations, we have learned to observe them without judgment or attachment. This ability to observe and accept our experiences has allowed us to develop a new relationship with our thoughts and emotions, freeing ourselves from their grip and finding a sense of liberation.

Moreover, this book has emphasized the importance of integrating mindfulness into our daily lives. Mindfulness is not limited to the moments we spend on the meditation cushion; it is a way of being. By infusing our everyday activities with presence and awareness, we can create a lasting shift in our perception of the world. From savoring a cup of tea to engaging in conversations, each moment becomes an opportunity for mindfulness and self-discovery.

Throughout our journey, we have discovered that self-compassion, patience, and non-judgment are vital companions on the path to healing. By extending kindness and understanding towards ourselves, we can navigate the ups and downs of life with greater resilience and self-acceptance. We have learned to approach our experiences with patience, knowing that healing takes time and

progress may be nonlinear. And by letting go of judgment, we have created a space where true transformation can unfold.

As we close this book, let us remember that its purpose has been to inspire hope, empowerment, and the possibility of finding inner peace and well-being through mindful meditation. No matter how deep the darkness of depression may seem, there is always a flicker of light within us waiting to be nourished. By dedicating ourselves to the practice of mindfulness, we have the potential to ignite that light, guiding us towards a life filled with joy, purpose, and deep healing.

May this book serve as a guide and companion on your journey towards inner peace. May it remind you that you are not alone in your struggles and that a path towards healing exists within your reach. With each breath, each moment of mindful awareness, you are taking steps towards a brighter, more fulfilling life.

May you continue to embrace the transformative power of mindful meditation, integrating it into the very fabric of your being. May you find solace, strength, and profound healing on this remarkable path. Remember, the seeds of inner peace and well-being reside within you, patiently waiting to blossom.

Thank you for joining me on this transformative journey. May your life be forever touched by the transformative power of mindful meditation.

ABOUT THE AUTHOR

Thomas has been a Buddhist practitioner for the past 26 years. He is a master of meditation and lives in Texas with his beloved dog Jake. Thomas enjoys running for health which he does mindfully. He is the author of ,"Mindfully Grounded: A Guide To Overcoming Anxiety Through Meditation" and "Paws Of Love: Navigating Pet Loss and The Path To Healing".

Other books by Thomas

Available on Amazon

Leave a 1-Click Review!

I would be incredibly thankful if you could take just 60 seconds to write a brief review on Amazon, even if it's just a few sentences!

>> Click here to leave a quick review